THE SEARCH FOR EXTRATERRESTRIAL INTELLIGENCE

Life Beyond Earth

Joe Rhatigan

Lerner Publications ◆ Minneapolis

Lerner Publications Company
An imprint of Lerner Publishing Group, Inc.
241 First Avenue North
Minneapolis, MN 55401 USA

For reading levels and more information, look up this title at www.lernerbooks.com.

Main body text set in Aptifer Sans Regular.
Typeface provided by Linotype.

Library of Congress Cataloging-in-Data

Names: Rhatigan, Joe, author.
Title: The search for extraterrestrial intelligence : life beyond Earth / Joe Rhatigan.
Description: Minneapolis, MN : Lerner Publications, [2024] | Series: Alternator books. Space explorer guidebooks | Includes bibliographical references and index. | Audience: Ages 8–12 | Audience: Grades 4–6 | Summary: "Are we alone in the universe? Scientists are searching and it's possible that one day we will know the answer. Full-color photographs and intriguing text invite the reader to become part of the search"—Provided by publisher.
Identifiers: LCCN 2023013555 (print) | LCCN 2023013556 (ebook) | ISBN 9798765609101 (library binding) | ISBN 9798765624951 (paperback) | ISBN 9798765617946 (epub)
Subjects: LCSH: Life on other planets—Juvenile literature. | BISAC: JUVENILE NONFICTION / Science & Nature / Astronomy
Classification: LCC QB54 .R395 2024 (print) | LCC QB54 (ebook) | DDC 576.8/39—dc23/eng20230714

LC record available at https://lccn.loc.gov/2023013555
LC ebook record available at https://lccn.loc.gov/2023013556

Manufactured in the United States of America
1 – CG – 12/15/23

TABLE OF CONTENTS

IS THERE ANYBODY OUT THERE?

Have you ever looked up at the night sky and wondered if there's something (or someone!) far, far away looking back in your direction? Perhaps they are wondering the same thing. Do you believe in unidentified flying objects (UFOs)? Or that aliens might visit and ask you to take them to your leader? Movies, TV shows, and books would have you believe that there are alien species in far-away galaxies. We have not yet found signs of life beyond Earth, but that does not mean we're not looking!

Scientists around the world study our planet, the other planets in our solar system, and star systems billions of miles away to attempt to answer the question: Are we alone in the vast universe?

TREASURE HUNT

Whether or not we share the universe with other life forms has interested humans for over two thousand years. Ancient Greek philosophers assumed there were other worlds filled with life. Since then, the search for extraterrestrial intelligence (known by the acronym SETI) has felt like a vast treasure hunt. Scientists use the latest technology, along with some strange outside-the-box ideas, hoping to find life on other worlds.

Ready to join the hunt?

The Hubble Space Telescope spotted a spiral galaxy shaped like a classic science fiction flying saucer. Astronomers named it the UFO Galaxy.

In 1947, a rancher found a "flying disc" on his property in Roswell, New Mexico. Early media reports that said it was a flying saucer were later proved false after extensive investigation.

UFOs!

On June 24, 1947, a pilot named Kenneth Arnold reported seeing nine objects in the sky. He said they flew like saucers skipping across the water. Since then, there have been thousands of sightings, and some people claim that they have even been abducted by aliens—and returned! So far, no UFOs have ever been confirmed as spaceships from another world, but there are many that are still unexplained.

CHAPTER 1

WHAT EXACTLY ARE WE LOOKING FOR?

Astrobiologists are scientists who study life on Earth and life in space. They are like detectives looking for clues that life exists or that it once existed on a different planet or moon. The clues can be big, such as finding water on a planet. They can also be small, like particles, which are tiny pieces of matter, discovered on a meteorite.

Astrobiologists study the origins of life on Earth, hoping to find clues about how life might exist elsewhere. They also search for signs of life using space probes and telescopes. They try to answer questions like, "Can life elsewhere be something completely different than life on Earth?" For example, can a life-form on another planet eat mercury for breakfast? Eating mercury would make humans very sick.

In 1971, scientists reported that they found amino acids, one of the building blocks of life, on a meteorite that crashed to Earth.

NASA's Transiting Exoplanet Survey Satellite (TESS) is a space telescope whose sole job is to find new planets that could have life.

WHAT ARE SIGNS OF LIFE?

Life needs just the right ingredients to exist. To start, living things need a source of energy. Here on Earth, for example, the plants that we eat need light energy to grow. Plants get this light energy from the Sun. So, scientists look for planets that orbit around a star like our Sun.

A planet with life needs to have a stable environment that's not too hot and not too cold. It needs an atmosphere, which is the gases that surround a planet. Within that atmosphere, there must be the right gases for life to exist, such as carbon, hydrogen, oxygen, nitrogen, and others. The planet must also have water, or at least ice or water vapor, for life to exist. These are some of the clues scientists look for.

Water is a necessity for life.

Tardigrades are nearly indestructible eight-legged microscopic animals that can live just about anywhere, including outer space.

CHAPTER 2

HERE ON EARTH

To help us find clues about what kind of life to look for, we start right here on Earth. Can life exist in total darkness? How about when there is very little water or oxygen? Scientists answer these questions by studying life on Earth that lives in extreme environments—places where humans would struggle to survive. For example, in the vent of an underwater volcano, scientists have discovered three hundred new microorganisms. Microorganisms are living things that you cannot see with your eye. They live 6,000 feet (1,829 meters) below sea level in fluid that is 600°F (320°C).

These organisms are called extremophiles. By studying them, we can begin to think about possible life-forms on planets where the environments are extreme. Mars or Jupiter's moon Europa are two such environments.

Scientists have discovered heat-loving microorganisms that can live in the acidic environments surrounding the geysers at Yellowstone National Park.

Water isn't a biosignature, but the seashells on shore are.

BIOSIGNATURES

When you write your name on a test, it shows that you took the test. If you see a branch on the ground, you can guess that there is a tree nearby. The branch is an example of a biosignature. A biosignature is anything that proves life is or was there. Scientists use biosignatures as clues. They can be things like fossils, atmospheric gases, or rocks. Since we cannot easily get these things from other planets, we study biosignatures here on Earth to help us find ways to identify them in space.

Fossils give us clues about things that lived in the past.

METEORITE CLUES

Scientists study meteorites to look for biosignatures or other signs of microscopic life, which is anything living that can only be seen with a microscope. So far, they haven't found any. However, they have found evidence of materials that could form life.

This has raised an important question: Is it possible that life on Earth began in space? Are *we* the aliens?

Meteorites come from asteroids as well as from Mars and the moon.

Dr. Carl Sagan was a famous astronomer who lived from 1934 to 1996.

Carl Sagan

Carl Sagan's interest in outer space began when he was five years old. He got his library card so he could find a book that would tell him what stars were. The answer amazed him and led him to become one of the world's most famous astronomers. His television show, *Cosmos*, opened the world of astronomy to millions of viewers, and his belief in the possibility of extraterrestrial life sparked the growth of astrobiology.

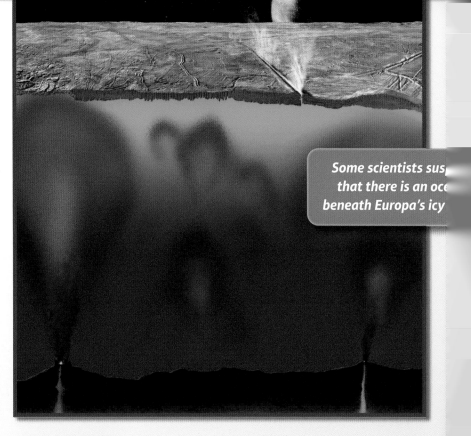

Some scientists susp[ect]
that there is an oce[an]
beneath Europa's icy [surface]

SEARCHING OUR SOLAR SYSTEM

Our solar system has seven planets in addition to Earth: Mercury, Venus, Mars, Jupiter, Saturn, Uranus, and Neptune. It also includes the Sun, dwarf planets (like Pluto), moons, asteroids, comets, and meteors. When searching our solar system for life, we look for either biosignatures or for conditions that might be right for life—such as liquid water or atmospheric gases, like oxygen. Scientists have narrowed their search to a few key planets and moons. With data from telescopes, rovers, probes, and fly-by space missions, they are getting closer to finding answers.

EUROPA

Europa, one of Jupiter's moons, is encased in a 15-mile-thick (24 km) shell of ice that covers a gigantic ocean. The underground water could contain life since the ocean is heated up by the movement of tides. The European Space Agency is launching the Jupiter Icy Moons Explorer to explore Jupiter and its moons. It will reach Europa by 2030.

Jupiter's moon Europa has a block-like crust.

MARS

People have wondered about whether or not there is life on Mars for more than one hundred years. Today, scientists focus more on whether there *used* to be life on Mars.

Millions of years ago, Mars had lakes, rivers, and water on its surface. The National Aeronautics and Space Administration (NASA) has sent five probes to the surface of Mars looking

Perseverance is the size of a small SUV. Its mission is to look directly for signs of past life on Mars.

A self-portrait of Curiosity drilling on Mars

for evidence of past life. Currently, the Perseverance rover is analyzing soil, rock, and air samples, looking for biosignatures of past or present life.

Meanwhile, the Curiosity rover, which has been studying Mars since 2012, has found a surprising amount of methane. Methane is a gas that is produced by microorganisms. This could be a clue that there is life on Mars. Future missions will help determine where the methane is coming from.

OTHER TARGETS

One of Saturn's moons, Titan, has a thick atmosphere and lakes of liquid methane and ethane. Scientists are studying both its atmosphere and surface looking for potential life. They are also analyzing geysers of water vapor that are erupting on Enceladus, another Saturn moon.

WHY DO WE KEEP GOING TO THE MOON?

There are lots of reasons NASA focuses so much attention on Earth's moon. For one thing, the moon formed from Earth. Studying moon rocks can give us a record of early Earth, before there was life. These rocks could hold the key to how life evolved here, which would then help us understand how life can evolve somewhere else.

Researchers continue to study moon rocks gathered by astronauts during the Apollo missions.

Traveling at a speed of 34,797 m (56,000 kph), it would take 81,000 to get from Earth to Proxima Cent

CHAPTER 4

EXPANDING THE SEARCH

The closest star to us (besides our Sun) is called Proxima Centauri. It is 4.25 light-years from Earth. That's about 25 trillion miles (40 trillion km). We won't be traveling there anytime soon. However, in 2020, the European Southern Observatory in Chile confirmed that a planet is orbiting Proxima Centauri.

EXOPLANETS

One of the most exciting recent developments in SETI is the discovery of exoplanets, such as the one orbiting Proxima Centauri. An exoplanet is a planet outside our solar system. Using telescopes, such as the recently launched James Webb Space Telescope, scientists have identified thousands of worlds, many of which could be perfect for life.

The James Webb Space Telescope was launched in 2021. So far, it is the most powerful space telescope ever built.

LISTENING CLOSELY

Radio waves send sounds or other information through the air and through space. We use radio waves to broadcast radio stations and cellphone calls. We also use radio telescopes to search for communication from distant worlds, with the hope that we can listen in. Radio telescopes are like giant antennas pointed toward the stars. They are bigger than telescopes that look for light, and usually look like giant dishes.

The National Radio Astronomy Observatory's Very Large Array radio telescope in New Mexico consists of twenty-seven antennas arranged in a huge "Y" pattern.

The Allen Telescope Array in California is the first telescope designed specifically for SETI uses.

SNOOPING ON ALIENS

Is there intelligent life in outer space? SETI astronomers are trying to find out using the Allen Telescope Array of forty-two radio antennas. These radio frequencies are tuned to "hear" the regions around twenty thousand red dwarf stars that are closest to Earth. Astronomers think that red dwarf stars might host planets that could be habitable. So far, the system has looked carefully at thousands of star systems. Is there life out there? Stay tuned!

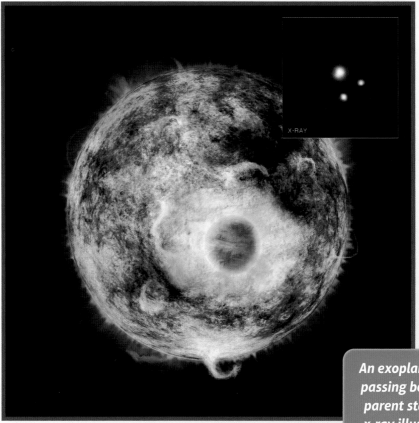

X-RAY

An exoplanet passing befo... parent star ... x-ray illustr...

THE HABITABLE ZONE

When searching for exoplanets, scientists look for worlds that are like our own: small, rocky, and just the right distance from a star so that liquid water can exist. Scientists call this perfect distance the habitable zone. In 2017, NASA announced it had found seven planets orbiting one star called TRAPPIST-1. Three of these planets are in the habitable zone. They could have water. They could have life.

WHAT THE FUTURE HOLDS

As exciting as discovering exoplanets is, these planets are too far away for us to find signs of water or biosignatures. However, using technology like the James Webb Space Telescope, we will soon be able to analyze these planets' atmospheres, and the gases they contain. This will help scientists zero in on planets that might have life.

Will we find microscopic organisms beneath the surface of Europa? Radio signals between two planetary systems? Life-forms creating methane trillions of miles away? Scientists hope that current and future technologies will bring us closer to figuring out whether we have neighbors in the universe.

James Webb Space Telescope in orbit near Earth

GLOSSARY

astrobiology: the study of and search for life on other planets

astronomer: a scientist who studies objects in space

extraterrestrial: not on Earth

extremophile: an organism that can survive in extreme environments

light-year: the distance light travels in one year, about 5.88 trillion miles (9.5 trillion kilometers)

meteorite: a rock from space that has fallen to Earth

microorganism: an organism that's too small to see with the naked eye

microscope: a tool with lenses used to magnify objects so they can be seen easily with the eye

orbit: the repeating path of an object in space moving around another object

probe: a device used to send back information from outer space

Britannica Kids: Extraterrestrial Life
https://kids.britannica.com/students/article/extraterrestrial-
life/274243

Goldstein, Margaret J. *Mysteries of Alien Life*. Minneapolis: Lerner
Publications, 2021.

Kenney, Karen Latchana. *Breakthroughs in the Search for Extraterrestrial
Life*. Minneapolis: Lerner Publications, 2019.

Krantz, Laura. *Is There Anybody Out There?: The Search for
Extraterrestrial Life, from Amoebas to Aliens.* New York: Abrams
Books, 2023.

NASA Kids' Club
https://www.nasa.gov/kidsclub/index.html

NASA Virtual Field Trips
https://astrobiology.nasa.gov/classroom-materials/

Warga, Jasmine. *A Rover's Story*. New York: HarperCollins Publishers, 2022.

Watch the Perseverance Rover Land on Mars
https://www.webcamtaxi.com/en/space/mars-
redplanetexploration.html

INDEX

PHOTO ACKNOWLEDGMENTS

Page 4-5; NASA, page 6; NASA/ESA/Hubble, page 7; iStockphoto/ DenisTangneyJr, page 8; US Department of Energy, page 9; NASA/Goddard Space Flight Center, page 10; Shutterstock/Jurga Jot, page 11; Shutterstock/fizkes, page 12; NASA/ Nicole Ottawa & Oliver Meckes/Eye of Science/Science Source Images, page 13; Shutterstock/Lane V. Erickson, page 14; Shutterstock/ Willyam Bradberry, page 15; iStockphoto/ Mypurgatoryyears, page 16; Shutterstock/Geermy, page 17; NASA/ "COSMOS• A PERSONAL VOYAGE "/ Druyan-Sagan Associates, Inc., page 18; NASA/JPL/ Michael Carroll, page 19; NASA, page 20; NASA/JPL-Caltech/MSSS, page 21; NASA/ JPL-Caltech, page 22; NASA/JPL-Caltech/Space Science Institute, page 23; NASA/MSFC History Office, page 24; ESA/Hubble & NASA, page 25; NASA, page 26; NASA/NRAO / AUI/NSF, page 27; SETI Institute, page 28; X-ray: NASA/CXC/SAO/K. Poppenhaeger et al; Illustration: NASA/CXC/M. Weiss, page 29; Shutterstock/Dima Zel.

Cover (image): Adobe/Frank Fichtmüller
Cover (background): Shutterstock/Maria Starovoytova
Interior background: Shuttesrstock/Sergey Nivens